Classic Tales

Level 2

C000143063

Big Baby Finn

Retold by Sue Arengo
Illustrated by Michelle Lamoreaux

 **Contents**

OXFORD

UNIVERSITY PRESS

 Here's Big Baby Finn. Big Baby Finn MacCool. And here's his friend Oonah. Clever little Oonah.

Finn and Oonah grow. They are friends. They like to play. They run and jump.

They jump into the river.

'Catch the fish, Oonah!' says Finn.

And she catches it. Clever Oonah catches the silver fish.

Today is Finn's birthday.

'Look!' cries Oonah. 'A gold fish! It must be magic!'

And the magic fish sings: 'Finn! Have this girl for your wife. She can help you in your life.'

Have this girl for your wife.

So Finn marries Oonah. They live on a green hill. And they can see the sea. The beautiful, big, blue sea.

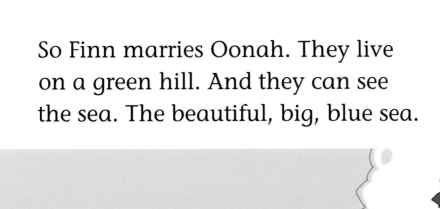

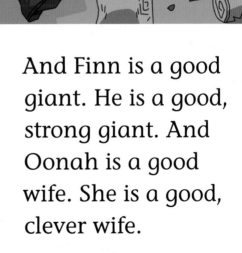

And Finn is a good giant. He is a good, strong giant. And Oonah is a good wife. She is a good, clever wife.

'OK, men!' says Finn. 'I want to make a bridge! A bridge across the water!'

Finn throws a big stone. Splash! Into the sea! And another! And another!

Splash! Splash! Into the sea!

'I am big and strong,' says Finn.
'I do good things.'

But then Finn sees something.
Something a long way across
the sea. And he doesn't like it.

'Oh! What is that?' he asks.

What is that?

7

'Oh!' say Finn's men. 'That's Big Bad Benan! With his bad magic finger!'

'Hey!' shouts Benan. 'I'm looking for Finn. Do you know him?'

'No!' shouts Finn.

'No!' say his men. 'No! We don't! We don't know Finn.'

'Help!' shouts Finn.

'What's the matter?' says Oonah.

'It's Big Bad Benan,' says Finn.
'He's coming for me!'

'Quick!' says Oonah. 'Make a cradle. Make a big baby's cradle. And bring it inside.'

'Now get in!' says Oonah. 'Get in the cradle! And don't say anything!'

They can hear Benan. They can hear Benan coming. And here he is ... Bang!

Where's Finn?

'Where's Finn?' shouts Benan.

'He's not here,' says Oonah. 'It's just me here. Me and the baby.'

'That's a big baby,' says Benan.

'Yes,' says Oonah. 'Just like his daddy. Finn is a very big giant. Much bigger than you!'

'Can you help me?' says Oonah. 'Can you turn the house, please? Finn usually does it. But he's not here.'

'OK,' says Benan. And he turns the house.

Then Oonah picks up some stones. And she puts them in her pocket.

Oonah is making bread.
She is making bread rolls.
But she has something.
She has some stones.

Oonah makes bread rolls. And she puts the stones in them. But … there is one with no stone.

'Mm!' says Benan. 'Those rolls smell good.'

'Here you are!' says Oonah.

There is a stone inside.

Benan starts to eat.

'Ow!' he shouts. 'What's wrong with this bread? Ow! My teeth!'

'Your teeth aren't very strong,' says Oonah. 'My Finn eats this bread every day.'

Then the baby starts to cry.

'What's wrong with the baby?' shouts Benan.

'He's hungry too,' says Oonah. 'Here, baby! Here's a bread roll for you.'
(It's the one with no stone inside.)

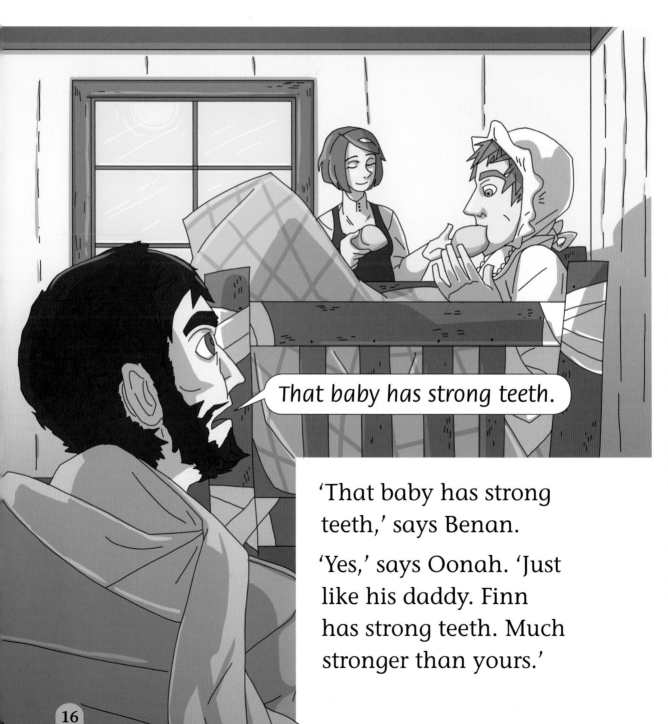

That baby has strong teeth.

'That baby has strong teeth,' says Benan.

'Yes,' says Oonah. 'Just like his daddy. Finn has strong teeth. Much stronger than yours.'

But the baby starts to cry again.

'Oh no!' says Oonah. 'Finn's coming home soon. He gets angry when the baby cries!'

'Be quiet, baby!' says Benan.

'Give him your finger!' says Oonah.

'Here, baby,' says Benan.

He puts his finger into Finn's mouth. His magic finger.

And Big Baby Finn bites it! He bites off the magic finger!

'Ow!' shouts Benan. 'Ow! Ow!'

And he gets smaller. He gets smaller and smaller!

Now Benan is tiny. Tiny, tiny Benan.
And tiny, tiny Benan … runs away.

'My clever Oonah!' says Finn.

'Goodbye, Benan!' says Oonah.

'Goodbye, Benan!' says Finn.

'Bye Bye!'

Exercises

1 Write the words.

~~clever~~ stronger big gold smaller

1 Oonah is ___clever___.

2 It's a _____ fish.

3 Benan is _____ than Finn.

4 He's a _____ baby.

5 Finn's teeth are _____ than Benan's.

2 Answer the questions. Write *Yes* or *No*.

1 Is Benan a good giant? _____No._____

2 Do the bread rolls smell good? _____Yes_____

3 Does Oonah give Benan a bread roll? _____yes_____

4 Is there a stone in the bread roll? _____

5 Does Benan get bigger and bigger? _____yes_____

3 Write the numbers and write the words.

Have   Get in   Give   ~~Catch~~   Make   Bring

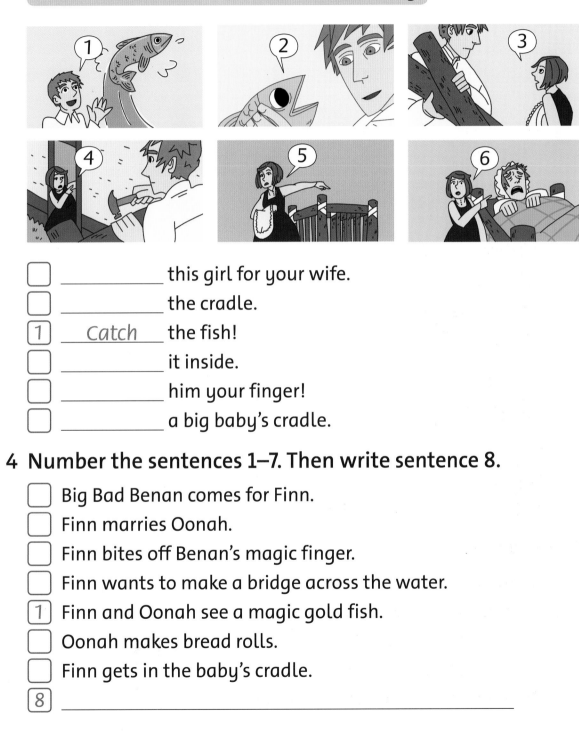

- [ ] _____ this girl for your wife.
- [ ] _____ the cradle.
- [1] _Catch_ the fish!
- [ ] _____ it inside.
- [ ] _____ him your finger!
- [ ] _____ a big baby's cradle.

4 Number the sentences 1–7. Then write sentence 8.

- [ ] Big Bad Benan comes for Finn.
- [ ] Finn marries Oonah.
- [ ] Finn bites off Benan's magic finger.
- [ ] Finn wants to make a bridge across the water.
- [1] Finn and Oonah see a magic gold fish.
- [ ] Oonah makes bread rolls.
- [ ] Finn gets in the baby's cradle.
- [8] _____

Picture Dictionary

birthday

bite

bridge

clever *She is clever.*

cry

finger

fish

giant

gold *a gold fish*

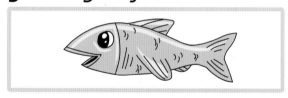

grow